BELONGS TO: